GW01158923

WEATHER FOR KIDS
PICTIONARY

GLOSSARY OF WEATHER TERMS FOR KIDS
CHILDREN'S WEATHER BOOKS

BABY PROFESSOR
EDUCATION KIDS

Speedy Publishing LLC
40 E. Main St. #1156
Newark, DE 19711
www.speedypublishing.com
Copyright 2017

All Rights reserved. No part of this book may be reproduced or used in any way or form or by any means whether electronic or mechanical, this means that you cannot record or photocopy any material ideas or tips that are provided in this book.

In this book, we're going to talk all about weather terms. So, let's get right to it!

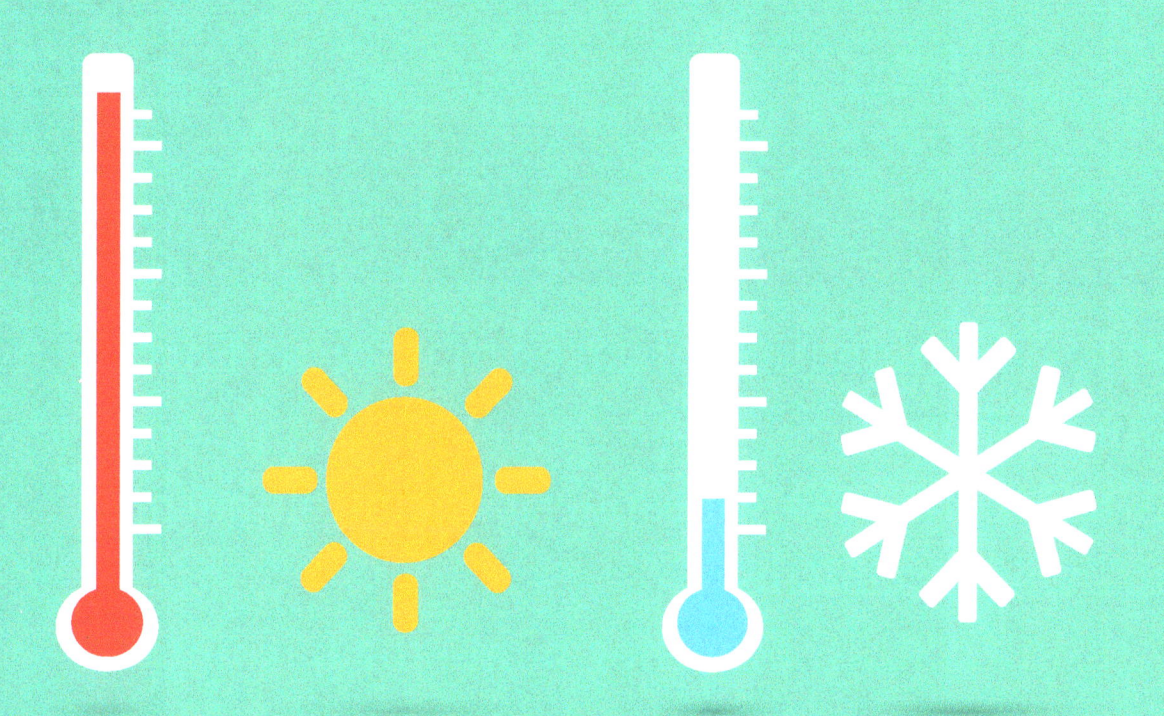

AIR: A combination of gases that forms Earth's atmosphere

AIR POLLUTION: Atmospheric chemicals harmful to living organisms

AIR PRESSURE: Another name for barometric pressure

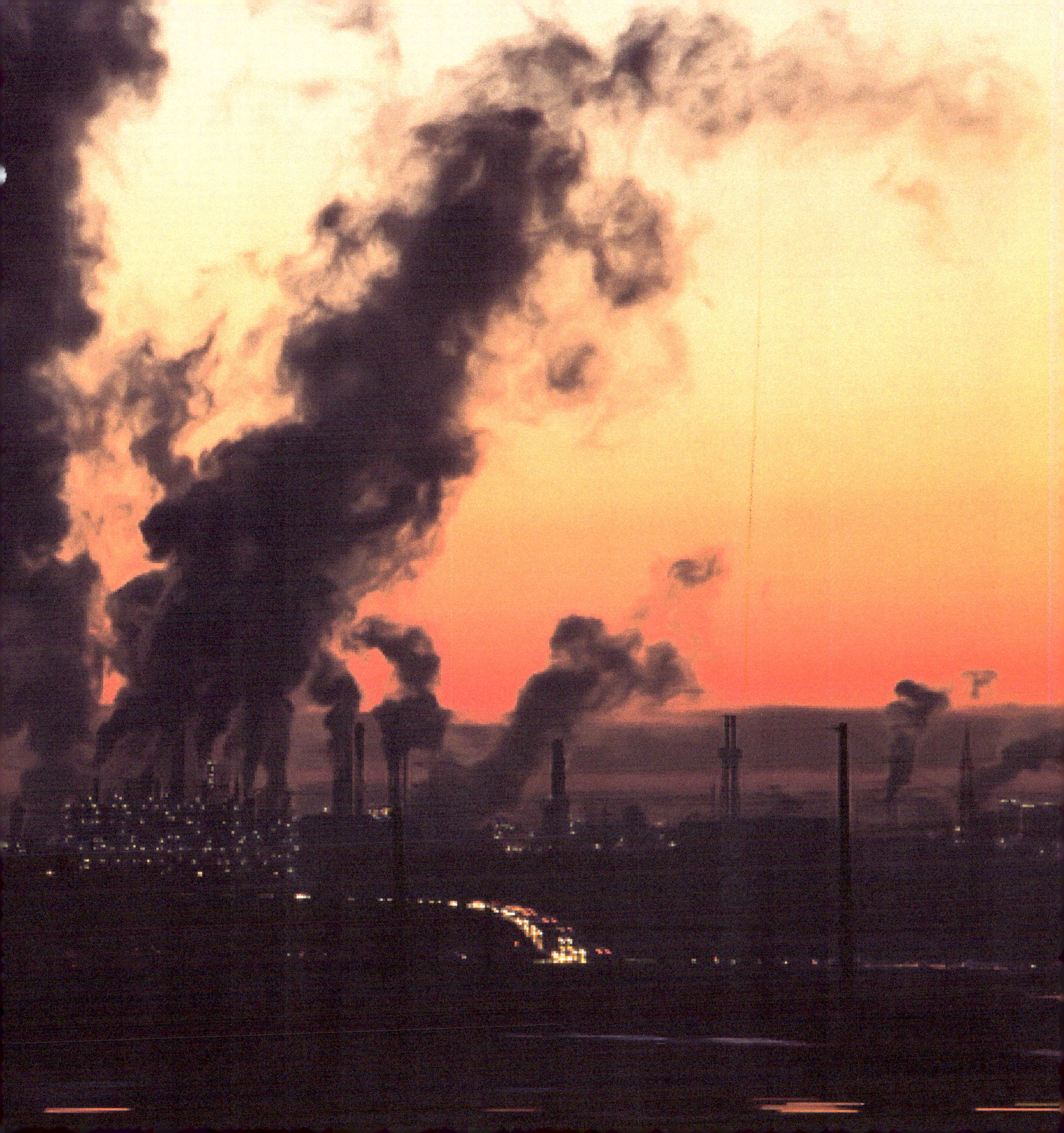

AURORA BOREALIS

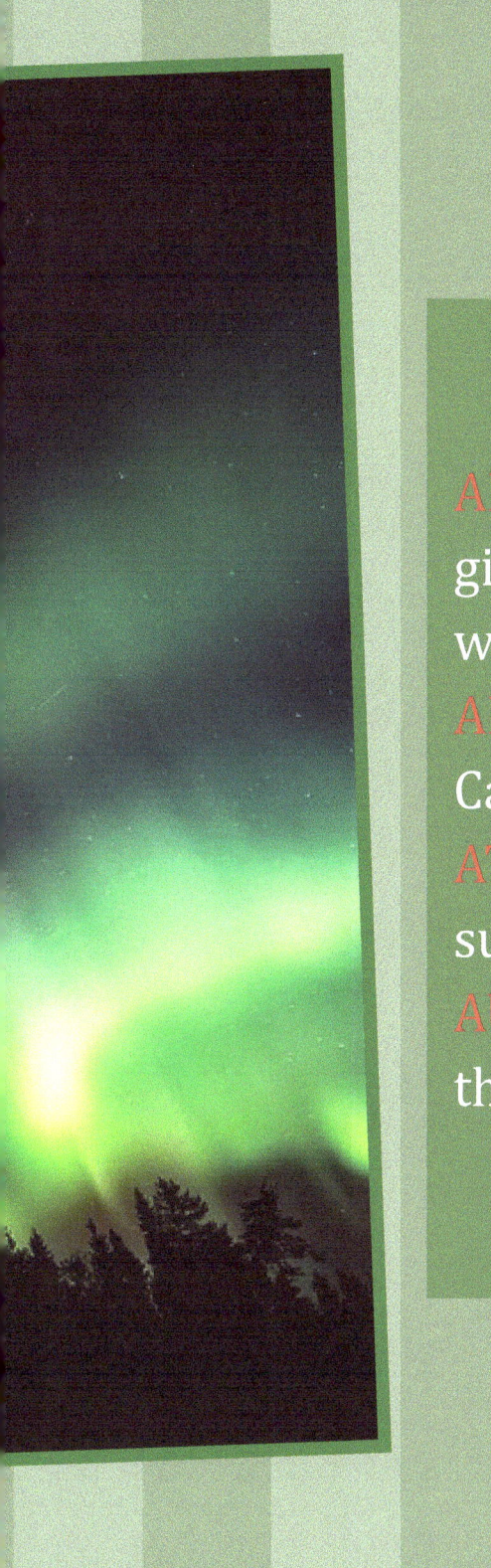

ANEMOMETER: A piece of equipment that gives a measurement for the speed of the wind

ARCTIC AIR: A mass of air that begins above Canada and creates cold temperatures

ATMOSPHERE: The mixture of gases that surrounds a planet

AURORA BOREALIS: Colorful lights above the Earth caused by a solar storm

BAROMETER: A piece of equipment that measures the pressure of the air

BAROMETRIC PRESSURE: The pressure created by Earth's atmosphere, which is the weight of the air

BAROMETER

BLIZZARD: A winter snowstorm that has intense 35 mile-per-hour winds
BREEZE: A slightly blowing wind

BLIZZARD

CIRRUS CLOUDS

CIRRUS CLOUDS: One of the major types of clouds, which form at high altitudes and look thin and wispy

CLEAR SKY: A sky that doesn't have any clouds

CLIMATE: The condition of the weather in a certain area over a long period of time

CLOUDS: Tiny droplets of water or ice crystals that collect in the atmosphere as different shapes

COASTAL FLOODING: Winds and tides combine causing rising sea levels that flood the coasts

COLD FRONT: The boundary where a cold air mass

FLOODING

and warm air mass meet with the cold replacing the warm

CONDENSATION: Water vapor transforming to liquid water and forming droplets such as dew

CUMULONIMBUS CLOUDS: One of the major types of clouds, they are dense and grow vertically creating thunderstorms and sometimes hail or tornadoes

CUMULUS CLOUDS: One of the major types of clouds, they are large, fluffy, positioned at mid-level in the atmosphere, and generally mean good weather

CYCLONE: A system of low pressure indicating a tornado, hurricane, or dust storm
DENSE FOG: Fog that decreases the horizontal view to less than ¼ mile, which causes travel delays
DEW: Water droplets on the surface of ground objects formed by atmospheric vapor
DRIZZLE: Rain composed of small droplets of water

CYCLONE

DROUGHT

DROUGHT: A long period of time characterized by little to no precipitation

DRY LINE: A boundary separating two masses of warm air, one dry and one moist, where thunderstorms often develop

DUST DEVIL: Small dust whirlwinds that form in desert areas

EL NIÑO: Warm currents of ocean water that develop off the coastlines of both Peru and Ecuador in late December, which cause destructive weather

EVAPORATION: The transformation of liquid water to vapor, which is a gas

FLASH FLOOD: Intense flooding that happens without any warning after severe rainstorms

FLOOD: When water spills over river banks from heavy rainfall

FOG: A cloud that travels at ground level reducing visibility

FOG

FREEZE: When the temperature decreases to below 32 degrees Fahrenheit for a period of time

FREEZING RAIN: Rain falling in droplets that freezes on the ground creating an icy glaze

FROZEN LEAVES

FRONT: The borderline between two varying masses of air that results in storms

FROST: White crystals of ice that cover a surface such as the soil or a plant's leaves

FUNNEL CLOUD: A tornado that never touches the ground's surface

GLOBAL WARMING: A scientific theory stating that Earth's temperatures are beginning to increase due to the level of greenhouse gases

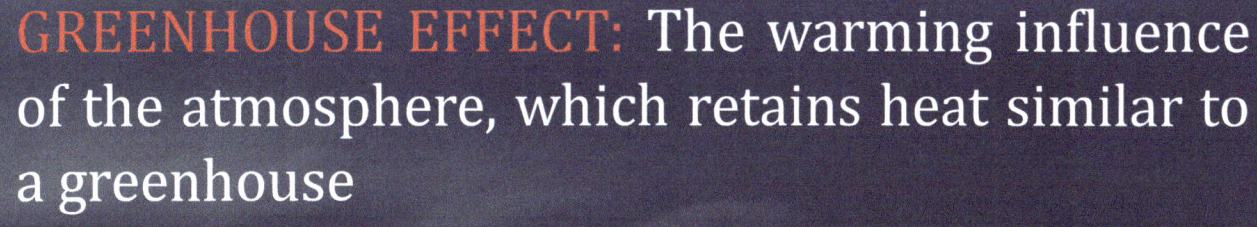

GREENHOUSE EFFECT: The warming influence of the atmosphere, which retains heat similar to a greenhouse

HAIL: Chunks of ice that fall in rain or freezing rain from cumulonimbus clouds

FUNNEL CLOUD

HAZE

HARD FREEZE: At least four hours in succession of temperatures 26 degrees Fahrenheit or lower, which destroys crops

HAZE: Tiny particles of pollution that are present in the atmosphere, which decrease visibility

HIGH PRESSURE SYSTEM: A swirling mass of air that is cool as well as dry, which brings light breezes and good weather

HUMIDITY: A measurement of atmospheric vapor

HURRICANE: Severe storms with an average width of 300 miles with winds that travel up to 150 miles per hour in a swirling pattern

HURRICANE SEASON: The period of the year from the 1st of June to the 30th of November when hurricanes develop

HURRICANE

HYGROMETER: A piece of equipment that measures the level of humidity

ICE: A solid form of water

ICE

INDIAN SUMMER

ICE STORMS: A storm with freezing rain that covers ground objects with dangerous sheets of ice

INDIAN SUMMER: A period of calm, warm weather in the fall occurring after a cold spell

INVERSION: An atmospheric layer where there is an increase in temperature as the height increases

JET STREAM: Winds that travel faster than 200 miles per hour and move air masses at the height from 6 to 9 miles above Earth's surface

LA NIÑA: Cold currents of ocean water that develop in the equatorial waters of the Pacific Ocean, which cause destructive weather, although not as destructive as those caused by El Niño

LIGHTNING: Bolts of very hot electricity in the atmosphere caused by thunderstorms

LOW PRESSURE SYSTEM: A swirling mass of warm air that's moist that generally results in strong winds and thunderstorms

METEOROLOGIST: A scientist who researches the weather and makes forecasts of future weather patterns

LIGHTNING

MIST: A form of fog with tiny water droplets suspended in air

MONSOON: Wind occurring in Asia that reverses direction from the summer season to the winter season and often brings huge amounts of rainfall

MIST

NIMBUS: Describes an individual cloud or cloud group from which there's rainfall

OVERCAST: A wide layer of clouds covering the entire sky

NIMBUS CLOUDS

> RADAR

OZONE: Oxygen with a slight chlorine smell, in the lower atmosphere it is a pollutant, but in the upper atmosphere it helps to prevent harmful radiation from ultraviolet light

PRECIPITATION: Water in either liquid or solid form that falls from clouds

RADAR: A piece of equipment that meteorologists use to see patterns of snow or rain

RAIN: Water drops that fall from clouds

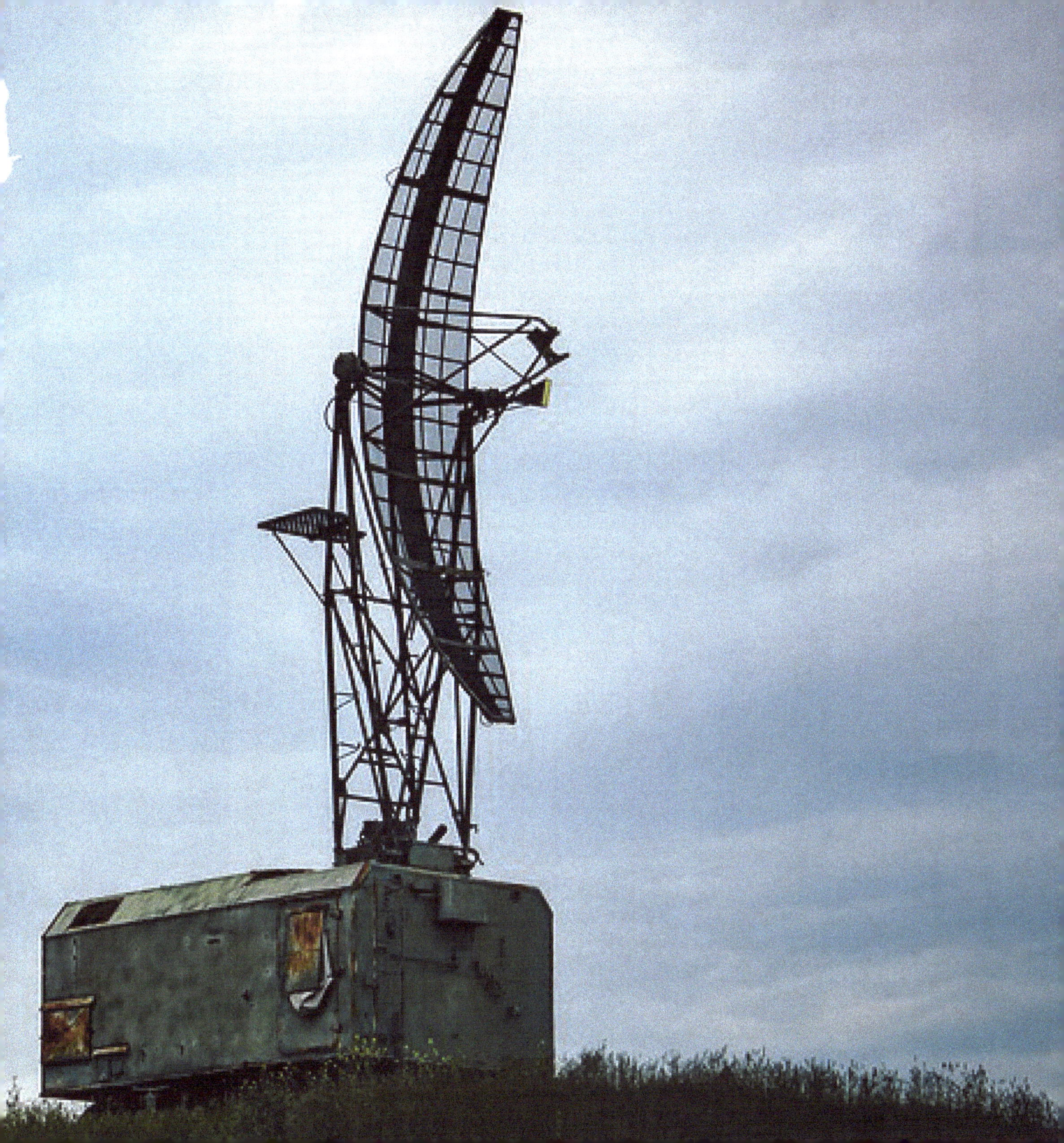

RAINBOW

RAINBOW: A spectacular arch of seven colors that is caused by the bending of sunlight through rain

RAIN GAUGE: A piece of equipment used to measure rainfall

RELATIVE HUMIDITY: The ratio of the amount of vapor held by the atmosphere compared to the largest amount it can hold at both that pressure and temperature

RIDGE: Long, narrow range of high pressure in the atmosphere

SANDSTORM: Strong winds that carry sand from sand dunes into the atmosphere

SEVERE THUNDERSTORM: Storms with winds higher than 58 miles per hour that often have hail pieces that are ¾ inch wide

SEVERE WEATHER: Any type of destructive weather

SLEET: Ice pellets that fall from the clouds, a type of precipitation

SANDSTORM

SLUSH: A soft, liquid mixture of snow mixed with ice and water on the ground

SMOG: Air pollution that can be seen in the atmosphere

SNOW: Water vapor that falls from clouds as frozen ice crystals in the form of light white flakes

SNOW ACCUMULATION: The depth of a snow layer on the ground

KID PLAYING IN THE SNOW

SNOW FLURRIES: Very small amounts of snow that don't accumulate on the ground

SNOWFLAKES: Ice crystals that have joined together in a hexagonal shape, no two are alike

SPRINKLE: A light rainfall that barely covers the ground

SQUALL LINE: Thunderstorms in a line that is hundreds of miles long

SNOWFLAKES

STRATUS CLOUDS

STABLE AIR: Air that resists movement in an upward direction since it is colder than surrounding air

STATIONARY FRONT: The borderline between two masses of air that remains in the same general location

STORM: An atmospheric condition that causes unpleasant weather such as thunder or lightning

STRATUS CLOUDS: A major type of sheetlike clouds that create drizzle and are low in the atmosphere and grey

SUBLIMATION: The process by which ice transforms into water vapor or vice versa without first changing to water

SUPERCELL: A supersized thunderstorm with updrafts in balance with downdrafts, which produce large-sized hail or tornadoes or both

TEMPERATURE: The measure of the atmosphere's level of cold or warmth

THERMOMETER: A piece of equipment that provides a measurement of temperature

THERMOMETER

THUNDER: The loud sound of the air as it expands due to lightning's intense heat

THUNDERSTORM: A storm that is composed of cumulonimbus clouds that emit thunder and lightning

TIDE: The systematic rise and fall of the level of water in the oceans caused by gravitational forces of the sun and moon on Earth

TIDAL RANGE: The variance in the level of water from high tide to low tide at a specific location

LOW TIDE

TORNADO: A funnel-shaped vortex of rotating wind that emerges from a storm system and strikes the ground causing destruction

TORNADO ALLEY: A section of the United States that has frequent tornadoes

TORNADO

TRANSPIRATION: The process by which plants emit water vapor into the atmosphere

TROPICAL STORM: A low-pressure atmospheric disturbance that forms over ocean waters in tropical regions with winds up to 73 miles per hour

TROPICAL STORM

TSUNAMI

TROPOSPHERE: The portion of the atmosphere closest to the Earth's surface where weather occurs

TROUGH: A long, narrow region of low atmospheric pressure

TSUNAMI: A very destructive ocean wave up to 200 feet in height that is caused by earthquakes or volcanic eruptions

TYPHOON: A hurricane over the western region of the Pacific Ocean

UNSTABLE AIR: Air that is warmer than its surroundings and tends to rise, leading to the formation of clouds and precipitation.

VISIBILITY: The distance a person can see through fog

WARM FRONT: The borderline between a cool air mass and one that's warm, moving so the warmer air displaces the cool air

WATER VAPOR: The gas form of water, which makes up no more than 4% of the atmosphere

WATER VAPOR

WHITEOUT

WATERSPOUT: A tornado that forms over a waterway

WEATHER: The air's condition and movement at a specific time as well as place

WHITEOUT: Severe conditions caused by a blizzard, which makes everything look white and is dangerous for drivers

WIND: Air movement relative to the Earth's surface

WIND CHILL: It's the "feel" of the temperature due to cold winds

SUMMARY

Once you read and study the terms in this Pictionary, you'll be able to better understand the daily weather forecast. Perhaps someday you'll study to become a meteorologist. Meteorologists are scientists who research and predict weather patterns.

Awesome! Now that you've read about weather terms you may want to read about the water cycle, which includes precipitation, in the Baby Professor book *Evaporation, Transpiration and Precipitation*.

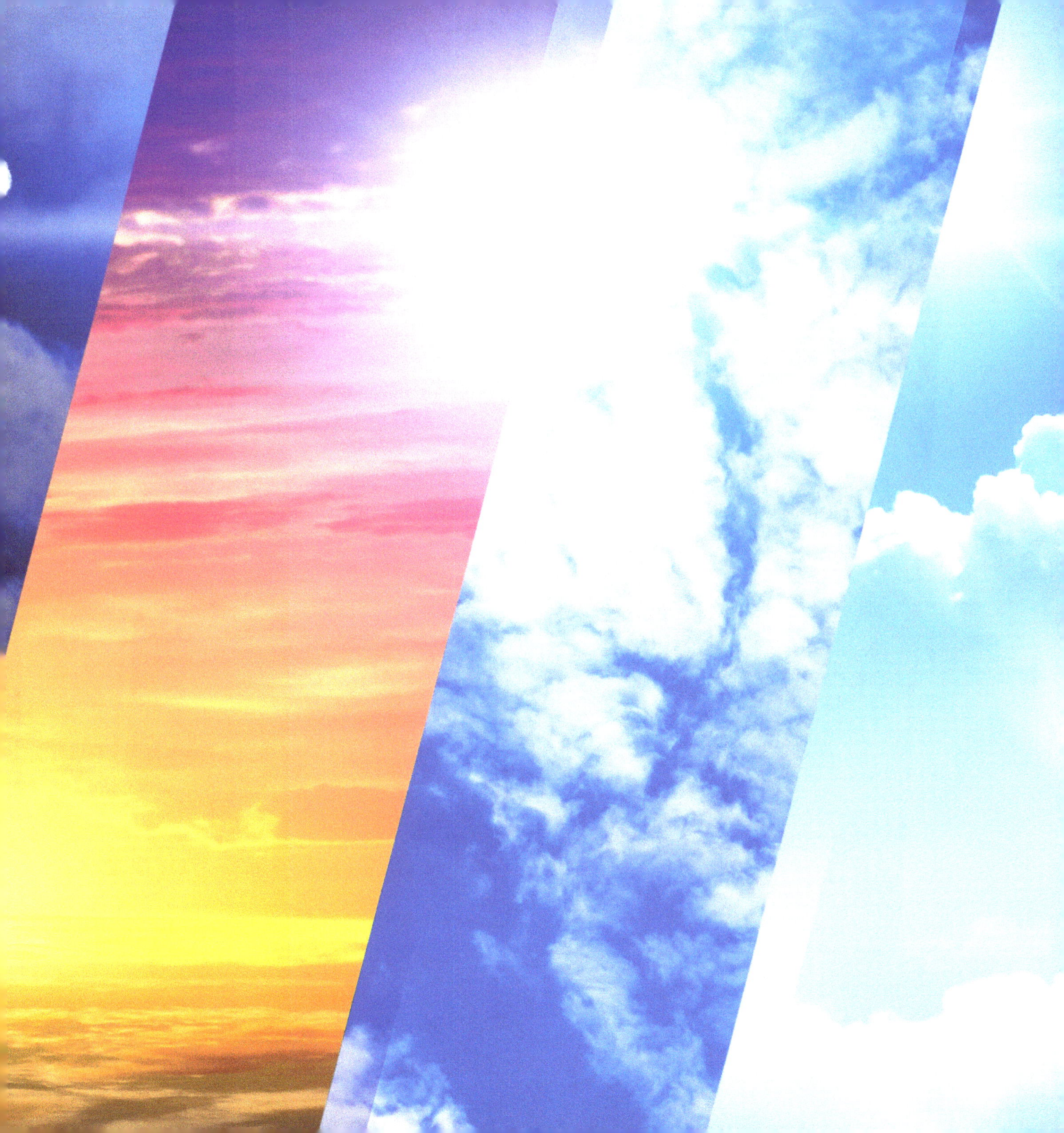

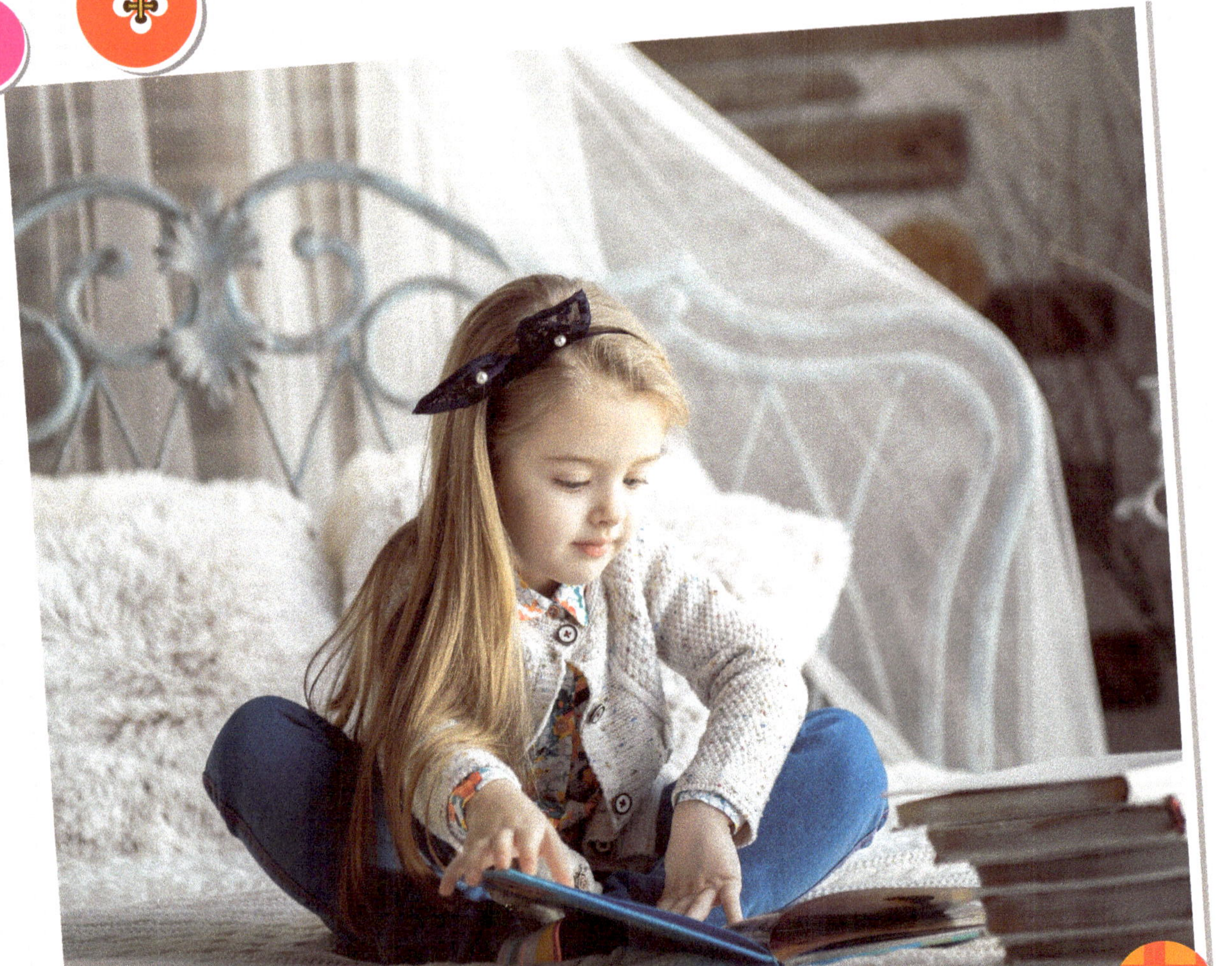

Visit

BABY PROFESSOR
EDUCATION KIDS

www.BabyProfessorBooks.com

to download Free Baby Professor eBooks and view our catalog of new and exciting Children's Books

Milton Keynes UK
Ingram Content Group UK Ltd.
UKHW050930310824
447642UK00002B/180